Cattle D

A Hands-on-History Look at the Cowboy of the 1800s West

Written by Robynne Eagan

Illustrated by Judy Hierstein

Teaching & Learning Company

1204 Buchanan St., P.O. Box 10
Carthage, IL 62321-0010

This book belongs to

_____

Dedicated to the wild horses that roam to this day.

Cover art by Judy Hierstein

Copyright © 2002, Teaching & Learning Company

ISBN No. 1-57310-351-9

Printing No. 987654321

Teaching & Learning Company
1204 Buchanan St., P.O. Box 10
Carthage, IL 62321-0010

Table of Contents

Resources 5

How It All Began/Imagine the Open Range 6

The Roundup 7

Make Your Own Lariat 8

How to Throw a Lariat 9

Branding 10

The Cowboy Alphabet/Common Figures and Picture Brands 11

Hands-On Brands 12

The Cattle Drive 13

Driving the Cattle 14

Trail Drive Play Station 15

Trouble on the Trail 16

The Cowboys Who Drove the Cattle 17

A Day in the Life of a Cowboy 18

Cowboy Culture 19

Get Your Hands on Tools of the Cowboy Trade 20

Tools of the Trade 21

These Boots Were Made for Riding 22

Cowboy Gear Matchup 23

Ride 'em, Cowboy! 24

Horse Sense 25

Cow Ponies 26

Cowboy Vittles 27

Day Is Done 28

What Would You Do at the End of the Trail? 29

The Rodeo 30

Come to the Cattle Drive 31

Cowboy Speak 32

Dear Teacher or Parent,

Saddle up and take your pardners on a ride through the history of cattle drives across the continent of North America. This short era has captured imaginations for generations, and your little cowpokes will be no exception.

Cattle Drive gives students the opportunity to immerse themselves in cowboy life on the trail with hands-on activities loaded with information and fun. They will find themselves in a time of rough, dusty trails winding through new territories, raucous roundups, wide open star-studded night skies and comradeship around a crackling campfire. They will learn to live like a cowboy on a cattle drive, dress for life on the trail, understand horse language, ride a cow pony, tie off a horse, lasso a longhorn, read and write a cow brand, organize a cattle drive and live it up cowboy style.

Through it all students will come to understand the factors that led to this epic adventure. They will visualize the wide-open range in a time before fences. They will understand how this open range filled with cattle and horses became important to growing cities of the east. They will study maps and mark trails, investigate transportation options of this era, discuss social implications of one's trade and come to know a group of hard-working and courageous pioneers who extended the boundaries of our nations.

Grab your Stetson and sit tight in your saddle for a ride through one of the most fascinating eras in North American history!

Sincerely,

Robynne

Robynne Eagan

Cattle Drive

Resources

Cowboy ABC by Chris Demarest. Dorling-Kindersley Publishing, 1999. (Ages 4-8)

Cowboys (Fact or Fiction) by Stewart Ross. Cooper Beech Books, 1995. (Ages 9-12)

Cowboys of the Wild West by Russell Freedman. Clarion Books, 1990. (Ages 9-12)

Cowboy Songs, Michael Martin Murphy, audio CD and audiocassette available, Warner Brothers (also Cowboy Songs 3 and Cowboy Songs 4).

Cowboy Songs, "Riders in the Sky," audio CD and audiocassette available, Easydisc.

Cowboy Songs of the Old West, Alan Lomax and Ed McCurdy, audio CD available, Legacy.

Cowboy Songs on Folkways, various artists (including Woodie Guthrie, Pete Seeger, Cisco Houston, Leadbelly and more), audio CD and audiocassette available, Smithsonian/Folkways.

In the Days of the Vaqueros: America's First True Cowboys by Russell Freedman. Clarion Books, 2001. (Ages 9-12)

The Journal of Joshua Loper: A Black Cowboy (My Name Is America series) by Walter Dean Myers. Scholastic, 1999. (Ages 9-12)

Trail Drive by James Rice. Pelican Publishing Company, 1996. (Ages 4-8)

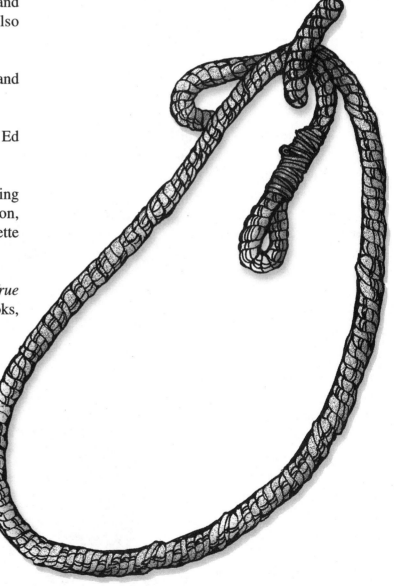

Cattle Drive

How It All Began

In the 1500s Spaniards reintroduced horses and brought longhorn cattle to North America. They set up ranches in Mexico and regions from Texas to California and in time their animals multiplied and wandered freely across these regions.

The first settlers to North America were largely homesteaders who provided for themselves but by the 1800s things were changing. Settlers and new immigrants were beginning to congregate in cities like Boston, Chicago, New York, Toronto and Montreal where shipping and industry created work. The shift from homesteading to life in industrialized cities created housing problems and difficulties in obtaining food.

Discussion

Where might city dwellers get their food? How is food transported today? What technology aids in the transport, storage and preserving of food today? In the 1800s there were no methods to refrigerate or move large amounts of food quickly to faraway locations.

Beef to the People

In the 1800s many people saw the demand for beef in the east and the promise of free or inexpensive land in the west as an opportunity to prosper. Thousands of settlers headed west to the wild cattle and open ranges. Cowboys were hired to take live cattle from the range to the city markets where they were sold and processed into beef. Some cowboys drove cattle further west and north to establish ranches on the open range that would be profitable when the coming railways linked the west and east.

Imagine the Open Range

The unsettled land of the west was an alluring new frontier. Wild and branded cattle wandered over great distances sharing grazing lands and water sources on the open range. It is estimated that there were once millions of cattle roaming the open ranges of North America.

Materials

atlas or large map of the Western frontier
historic photos of the open range of the 1800s

What to Do

1. Use the atlas and photos to take a look at the area discussed when it was a wide-open range.

2. Have students close their eyes and try to imagine what it would be like to see open range as far as the eye could see.

3. View pictures of these locations today. Discuss the changes.

Take a Look

Study old photographs of the wide-open ranges from a time not so long ago. Ask students to think about what life would have been like. How would they feel if they lived in a place like that? How has their area changed from the time when it was wide-open territory?

Cattle Drive

The Roundup

Before cattle could be driven to a new place they had to be rounded up. Twice a year cowboys herded cattle together in what was called a roundup. They counted new calves, checked brands, branded young cattle and selected the biggest cattle for the drive to market.

Longhorns

Colonists from the east brought English cattle to the continent. These mixed with the wild Spanish cattle to produce the hardy Texas longhorn. These cattle were lean, fast, strong, bad-tempered and easily spooked, and they had a set of horns that could grow to six feet across.

Lariat

A coil of rope was one of a cowboy's most important tools. With a few twists and knots the rope became a lariat that could help rope calves, cattle or horses for branding, taming or herding.

Lasso a Longhorn

A cowboy had to be quick and steady on his horse and good with a lariat to round up longhorn. These animals were known to charge when provoked and scared. Angry cattle with long, sharp horns could be a real threat. When a cowboy needed to catch a longhorn, he roped it with his lariat. It took a great deal of skill for a cowboy to twirl the rope over his head and send it over the horns or around the back legs of a longhorn while riding his horse. When a roped cow tried to pull away, the cowboy's horse braced itself and added resistance to the rope. As the loop tightened, the longhorn was held steady or pulled to the ground. The cowboy could then lead it or bring it to the ground for branding, inspection or to treat an injury.

Cattle Drive

Make Your Own Lariat

You can make a lariat and learn to toss it as the cowboys did. It's a bit tricky but can be done by children.

Materials

12-foot (3.6 m) length of ³/₈" (1 cm) thick manila cord (from hardware store) per lariat (adjust the length based on the height and arm length of each child)
plastic electrical tape
scissors

What to Do

1. Fold one end of rope back about 3" (7.5 cm) to form an eye. Wrap electrical tape around the base of the doubled cord to hold it in place. This little loop is called the "honda." (You can make overhand knots in place of electrical tape if children are good with knots.

2. Fold a section of the rope below the honda in half and thread it through the honda to create a loop or noose and you will have your lariat.

Roping Station

Set up a "calf" using poles standing in buckets of hardened cement, plaster or sand. Mark a line about 6' (2 m) from the pole. Invite students to try their hand at roping the "pole-calf" using a lariat.

Cattle Drive

How to Throw a Lariat

1. Before teaching students to throw, they must learn to properly coil a rope. Have children hold the rope in one hand and hold the other empty hand palm up ready to hold the coiled rope. Have children carefully loop the rope to form 12" (30 cm) loops over the other hand. Illustrate how giving the rope a half turn towards oneself while looping the coils will prevent the rope from twisting and kinking.

2. Now have students lay the rope out on the ground and work with one end. Demonstrate how to pull a loop through the honda until it is about 4' (1.2 m) in diameter.

3. Have students hold this loop in their right hand with the honda hanging about half way down on the side away from them.

4. Have students coil the excess rope gently in their left hand leaving about 6' (1.8 m) of loose rope between the coil and the loop.

5. Instruct students to hold the loop with the right hand about 1' (30 cm) from the honda and with the same hand grasp the rope about 1' (30 cm) below the honda.

6. Have students relax their wrists as they swing the loop up and overhead with a right to left motion. The wrist becomes the axle, the rope the wheel turning horizontally around the wrist and over the head. This is the wind up.

7. As the swinging hand comes from back to front, students should step forward as though throwing a baseball, bring the hand forward, palm down, to about shoulder level and then extend the arm and release the rope. If all goes well, the rope will sail towards the target.

Branding

American ranchers learned from the Spaniards how to mark animals so they would be easy to identify as their own during the roundup. A mark of ownership, called a brand, was burned onto the hide of an animal using a hot iron. These brands would mark an animal for life.

Every ranch had its own name and its own brand. The Spaniards used intricate brands, but the cowboys of North America created simple marks that were easy to make, read and remember. Brands could consist of letters, numbers and/or shapes.

Brands were (and still are) registered to livestock owners so lost or stolen animals can be easily identified. States and provinces have different rules regarding registered brands. As a general rule, brands are made of one, two or three figures that are clear and easily read. They usually represent objects familiar to the cowboy.

There are two types of branding irons. The stamp iron is a complete brand, forged all in one piece. It is heated and stamped onto the animal. A running iron was like a hot poker that was used to draw brands on a hide. This iron was eventually outlawed, as this method made it too easy for rustlers to change existing brands.

How to Read a Brand

Reading brands was simple for cowboys who recognized the symbols and knew the tricks to reading them.

Rules of Direction

1. From left to right
2. From top to bottom
3. From the outside to the inside

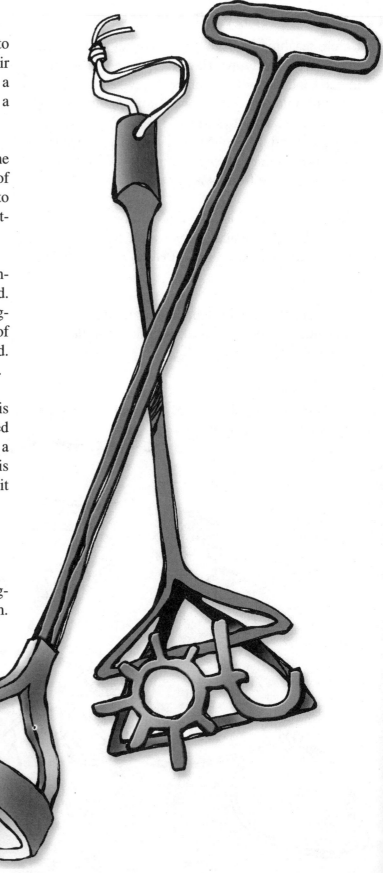

The Cowboy Alphabet

The rules below apply to numbers and letters of the alphabet.

1. Letters in their normal positions are pronounced by name. B
2. Letters slanted or tipping over are called "tumbling _____." *B*
3. A letter lying on its back is called "lazy _____." ⌐
4. A letter that is upside down is called "crazy _____." ⌐
5. A letter facing the wrong direction is called "reverse _____." ᙍ
6. A letter on a quarter circle is read "rocking _____." B
7. If a letter has wings, it is read "flying _____." ⇒B
8. If a letter has feet, it is read "walking _____." B
9. A letter in cursive is called "running _____." *B*
10. If the letters spell a word, then you read the word. BOB
11. Letter "O" is read as "circle"—i.e. OR is "circle R"
12. Zero can be used in a number, i.e. 101, 900, but on its own is "circle."

Common Figures and Picture Brands

Swinging	Ⓑ	Rocking	⊍B⊍
Bar	—	Diamond	◇
Half circle	⌒⌣	Half moon	☾
Buckle	▭	Spur	✪
Sun	☀	Sunrise	☀

As well as the simple marks provided here, cowboys created brands using many things that were a part of their day-to-day life including horns, horseshoes, skulls, the Bible, a pitchfork and initials.

Hands on Brands

Some letters cannot be crazy or upside down because when you change them in these ways they become another letter or stay the same. Can you guess which letters these might be? (X, I, H, O)

Concentrate and then read the following brands correctly:

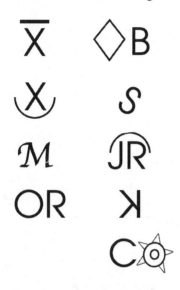

Design Your Own Brand

Use symbols you have learned to design your own brand.

Materials

pipe cleaners   bowl
paint   template for longhorn cow
heavy paper   scissors

What to Do

1. Design a simple brand.

2. Bend the pipe cleaner into the shape of your brand.

3. Add a second pipe cleaner to give your stamping brand a handle.

4. Dip your brand in the paint, blot it gently on test paper and then "brand" your page, or your work. Use your personal brand to mark your work throughout this unit.

Try This

Put together a "brand log," as a branding inspector would do. An inspector would not grant a brand that was too similar to another brand.

Leather Craft

Materials

leather swatches   leather-tooling stamps
leather-burning tool

What to Do

1. Invite students to stamp designs onto their leather pieces.

2. Punch holes on either side of the top. Thread the lacing through and then tie off so the leather creation can be hung up to display.

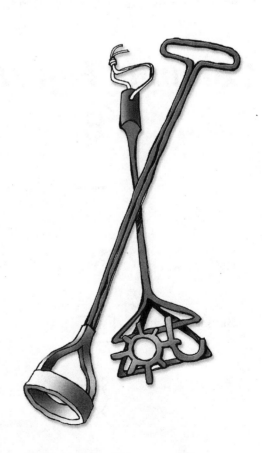

Cattle Drive

The Cattle Drive

Between 1866 and 1886 the drives were at their greatest number and the trade in cattle was booming in North America. Thousands of cattle were driven thousands of miles over uncharted terrain. Ranchers prospered as hardworking cowboys drove the cattle to the ranches, markets and railheads from where they would be shipped to markets in places like London, New York and Chicago. The business of moving cattle became an epic venture that would go down in history.

The first drives were short, safe trips along established trails, but as the trade in cattle increased and railways extended further into the west, there was a need to bring cattle from further afield and to more remote ports. Sometimes cattle were driven clear across the country to stock new ranches in the north or far west. Some were driven from Texas to establish ranches in Kansas, Wyoming, Montana, Missouri, the Dakotas and Canada.

Map It Out

Initially set up as a Civil War supply route, The Chisholm Trail between Texas and Kansas was one of the most popular and probably the most famous of the cattle trails heading to Abilene, Texas. Invite students to follow this (or another) trail on a copied map, an overhead or an atlas.

Abilene

The **Chisholm Trail**

San Antonio

Cattle Drive

Driving the Cattle

Cowboys took advantage of the longhorns instinct to stay together. A handful of cowboys could drive an entire herd hundreds, sometimes thousands of miles over all kinds of terrain. There were no roads or bridges—just rough trails created by the hooves of cattle. From sunrise to sunset herds of cattle tramped through all kinds of weather to get from one place to another. Cattle could cover, at the most, 15 miles (24 km) a day. Trips could last months.

About 10 cowhands were needed to drive 1000 head of cattle. They rounded up, roped, branded, herded and drove the cattle. Each had a specific task on the trail. They were positioned around the herd to keep the cattle moving in the right direction. They had to watch the cattle carefully, as they could be fast, ornery and easily spooked into starting a stampede.

A lead cowboy, or trail boss, was in charge of the drive. He rode out ahead of the herd, called to the cattle and looked for the next camp.

Point riders led the herd. They came to know and work with the longhorn leaders. They sometimes gave these lead steers names. The big steers called to the herd by bellowing and swinging their heads from side to side. Once the leaders were moving, the rest of the cattle would follow in a pack or straight line and the drive was underway.

Swing riders rode alongside the cattle to keep them moving in the right direction. Cattle didn't really like to walk long distances and would sometimes try to escape and run for home.

Flank riders rode up and down beside the line of cattle to make sure the herd didn't spread out too much.

Drag riders hung back to keep the cattle moving and to make sure none were left behind.

The wrangler rode along with the "remuda," or small herd of back-up horses. He made sure they were always ready to replace tired trail horses. He cared for all of the saddle horses and helped with camp chores.

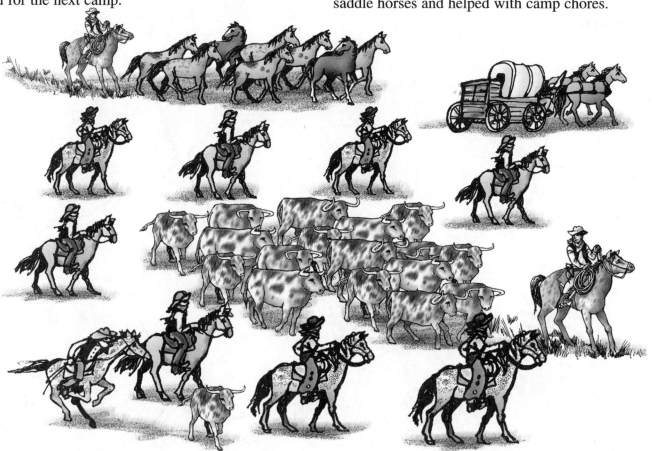

14

Cattle Drive

Trail Drive Play Station

Help students to better understand the logistics of the trail drive by placing three-dimensional models on a three-dimensional terrain.

Materials

photographs of cattle drives

variety of art supplies as needed for the model-making options

models that can be played with and moved to create different scenarios:

> magazine or photograph cut-outs on cardboard backing for paper-doll style cowboys, horses, cattle, trees, cacti
>
> self-hardening clay for models of people, animals and objects
>
> inexpensive plastic models purchased from a toy store

terrain base made of sturdy cardboard, Plexiglas™ or plywood, to be covered with . . .

> laminated photographs or magazine pictures
>
> clay or plasticine
>
> papier-mâché or flour and water for texture, and paint for color
>
> tissue paper or colored cellophane for rivers
>
> stones for boulders and glue sprinkled with sand or fine gravel

What to Do

1. Invite students to study photographs of trail drives. Talk about the terrain, the cattle, the horses and the positions of those on the drive.

2. Have students attempt to prepare models to a similar scale selected for the size of model you desire to make (or present plastic models to show scale for the landscape they will create).

3. Have students plan and create a sturdy landscape on the board supplied. You may group students to work on various aspects of the terrain.

4. Draw an overhead view of the usual formation of the trail drive. Talk to students about the various positions as you draw this example.

5. Invite students to put the details together when all elements are ready.

Prepare to Hit the Trail

Ask students to prepare lists of gear and clothing they might need if they were cowboys joining a cattle drive. Ask them to think about what they would be doing and how they would carry their gear.

Cattle Drive

Trouble on the Trail

Stampedes

Cattle would stampede when startled by wild animals or sudden noises, like thunder or gunfire. The ground shook as they ran wildly in all directions bellowing with terror. Brave cowboys tried to reach the front of the herd, shouting and shooting to get the leaders running in a circle until calm.

Rustlers

Cattle thieves, known as rustlers, jumped herds to cause stampedes. They rounded up and drove off as many cattle as they could in the chaos.

Mud

Cattle could become stuck in the mud (or snowdrifts) and panic. Cowboys roped these cows and tried to calm them down.

Injuries

When cowboys, horses and cattle were injured or became ill along the trail, cowboys did their best with limited medical supplies and knowledge.

River Crossings

Herds often had to cross wide rivers. A few cowboys led the way and cattle followed, often with only the tips of their noses and horns breaking the surface. Many cowboys couldn't swim and held tightly to their horses during the crossing. Panic and chaos sometimes broke out.

Crossing Territories

When cattle trails crossed Indian territories, natives sometimes charged a toll to allow the cattle to graze, trample and cross their land. The exchange was usually peaceful. Outlaws and others sometimes demanded tolls or tried to block passage and violence occasionally occurred.

Spreading of Disease

Some northern settlers forbade longhorns from crossing their lands. Longhorns were immune to, but carried ticks that spread deadly tick fever to other cattle.

Mother Nature

Severe storms with thunder and lightning, mud, floods and, in some cases, snow caused stampedes, endangered lives and killed the cattle's food.

The Cowboys Who Drove the Cattle

Create a Cowboy Profile

What traits do you think a cowboy would need to do his job? Make a list.

Hired horsemen who blazed trails across the continent were tough, agile, hardworking, self-reliant, courageous and loyal. They lived a life-style beyond the comforts of civilization and could adapt to almost any conditions. They took great pride in the work that set them apart from most of society. The unique cowboy traditions of the North American Wild West were a blend of experiences adopted and adapted from the Spanish-influenced vaqueros, and British and African cowhands.

Almost all cowboys were men, some looking for a way to leave home, some runaway soldiers, some farmers or settlers looking for adventure. They were Americans, Europeans, Native Americans trained by vaqueros and African Americans who had been slaves. The strict social expectations of the era kept most women and girls off the range until the end of the cattle drives. Life on the open range attracted many, but the harsh realities of the work saw the majority of would-be cowboys head for home.

Myths in the Making

Some saw cowboys as dangerous rogues who could not be trusted—they drank too much, owned too little and were dirty and tough. As the cowboy way of life began to disappear, he became a kind of national hero who symbolized the values and traits of freedom, honesty, independence, self-reliance, individualism, loyalty and hard work. Writers and artists began to portray the cowboy in a nostalgic way that emphasized his finer qualities. Painters, writers, musicians and moviemakers created a romantic myth about North American cowboys and the Wild West that is generally not historically accurate.

Make a Wanted Poster

Pretend you are a rancher looking for cowhands to drive your cattle to a railhead town. What traits do you think are important? Make a "wanted poster" to help you find the right cowhand for the job.

Make a traditional "wanted poster" to portray a law-breaking cowhand who personifies the nasty traits often associated with cowhand drifters.

A Day in the Life of a Cowboy

A cowboy's work was difficult, tiring, dangerous and sometimes monotonous. He would ride thousands of miles across all kinds of terrain and in all kinds of weather. He slept under the stars, faced cattle rustlers, stampedes and storms. He socialized around the campfire and would risk his life for a friend—be it his horse or another cowboy. He had to ride well, handle cattle and be able to withstand many unexpected challenges and hardships. Cowboys were paid very little but chose this life-style anyway.

Materials
brown paper bag
felt-tipped marker or quill pen

What to Do

1. For homework, have students crumple a brown paper bag over and over until it resembles soft old parchment.

2. Have students choose which cowboy they would like to be on a cattle drive (p. 14). Have them research what kind of work they would do on the trail (p. 14) what dangers they would face (p. 16), what they would eat (p. 27), what they would wear (p. 20) and what a typical day might be like.

3. Once they have compiled this information, have students write a rough copy of a letter they might write to family or a friend if they were on the trail.

4. Have students write the good copy on the parchment paper using a felt-tipped marker or a real inkwell and quill pen.

5. Invite students to share the letters with one another and put them on display for your culminating cowboy activity.

The Wild West

In the mid 1800s the west really was wild. Native peoples were not happy about losing their lands, freedom and food supply; herds of longhorn and the wild grasslands were there for the taking and there were none or few to keep the peace or enforce the law.

Cattle Drive

Cowboy Culture

Cowboy culture has captured imaginations for generations.

Cowboy Art

Artists Charles Russell and Frederic Remington recorded accurate details of life in the wild west before it disappeared. In 1881 Remington embarked on a mission to record a way of life that was disappearing. Later artists created works based on memories, second-hand stories or romanticized ideals.

- Expose your students to cowboy art to help them understand what life was really like. Visit an art gallery or museum, or study prints in fine books.

- Invite students to look very closely at the details captured in paintings. Ask students to talk about what various details convey about cowboy life. Can the students find clues that tell what the cowboys were doing? Where they slept? What they ate? How they were feeling or what they might have been thinking about? How the cattle or horses were treated?

Cattle Drive Mural

Have students paint a mural that depicts life on a cattle drive. Encourage students to include as many details as possible to capture the event and the animals and people who were part of it. Use the mural as a backdrop.

Tall Tales

Cowboys told stories through tales, songs, writings and poems. Cowboys and cowboy-wannabes used the era as inspiration for poetry, stories, songs, theater, movies and sideshows. There is even a separate category for westerns in literature.

- Share historic and modern stories, songs and poems about life on the trail.

- Find a cowboy poet to share his or her work with your class.

- Invite students to prepare a story to tell around the campfire.

- Invite students to write a poem about life on the trail. You may provide a poetic framework or allow free verse. Work on word lists, offer photos or poem starters to get young cowpokes writing.

  My good old hoss is my best friend . . .
  The cattle are restless today . . .
  We are tired and dusty . . .
  There are many miles yet to go . . .

- Have children print a final copy onto a cut-out cowboy hat. Post the hats on a bulletin board with the caption "Hats off to You, Pardner."

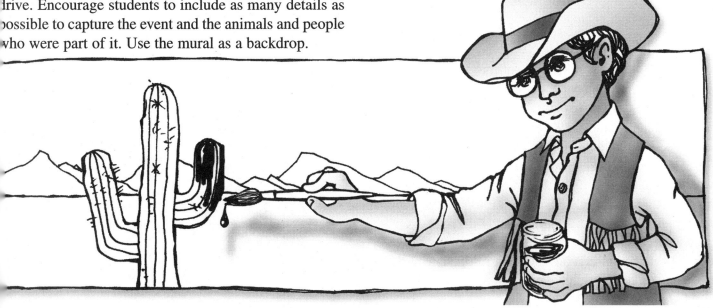

Cattle Drive

Get Your Hands on Tools of the Cowboy Trade

Provide students with firsthand exposure to tools of the trade that will bring the cattle drive to life.

Materials

borrowed items related to life on the trail (you can borrow many items from local museums or historians or from modern-day riders, blacksmiths or horse stables) or rely on models, posters or photographs of the items you cannot find.

cowboy hat	horse bridle
pair of spurs	branding iron
shirt	lariat
rope halter	horseshoes
pair of cowboy boots	canteen
chaps	saddlebag
bedroll	bandanna
western saddle	

What to Do

Discuss the cowboy's tools of the trade.

1. Invite children to discuss features of each item; texture, weight, durability and material.

2. What do children think the items were used for? Is the item still in use today? If so, how does the modern version differ?

Cowboy Clothing

Cowboys dressed in practical clothing for the job they did. Their clothing was comfortable, practical and durable providing protection from the hot sun, the cold, blowing dust, fierce winds and thorny underbrush and cacti. Although the Californian vaquero wore flashy Spanish dress, most cowboys relied on any practical wear they had for the job. Materials and specific clothing varied between seasons and regions. Patched denim jeans, shirts, chaps, leather boots and oilskin slickers for protection against rain and snow were common. Over time a distinctive cowboy style developed which has been passed down to this day.

Cattle Drive

Tools of the Trade

The Western Saddle

The most important and expensive piece of equipment a cowboy owned was his saddle. The western saddle evolved from the vaquero saddle to meet the needs of the working cowboy. It weighed between 30 and 50 pounds, had a deep seat, a high cantle or backrest and long wide stirrups to protect the cowboy and keep him balanced over the horse's back. A large pommel or horn and double girth was useful when roping cattle. A saddle pad went between the saddle and the horse to protect the horse's back.

Versatile Accessories

Many items worn by a cowboy had more than one use. Invite students to think of possible uses for basic cowboy gear listed on page 20.

Bandanna

A bandanna could be pulled over a cowboy's nose and mouth to keep out dust, tied over his hat to keep it in place, soaked in water and placed in the hat on hot days, placed to keep ears warm or used as a water filter or bandage.

Hat

The cowboy hat is a well-recognized symbol of the men who drove cattle. It was adopted from the vaquero sombrero and then adapted for working cowboys by John Stetson in the 1870s. It was made of stiff hair or felt that could be shaped to create just the right look. The brim and crown protected the cowboy from the sun, rain and cold, and the hat could serve as a pillow or drinking trough when necessary.

Knife and Revolver

Revolvers and knives had many uses on the trail. The revolver was used for protection on the trail and to deal with badly injured animals. It could be fired into the air to redirect a stampeding herd or as a call of distress. An all-purpose knife could be used for repairs, protection, meals or whittling.

LC10351 Copyright © Teaching & Learning Company, Carthage, IL 62321-0010

Cattle Drive

These Boots Were Made for Riding

Design a Boot

Before discussing traditional cowboy boots, have students design a boot of their own that would be well suited to life on the cattle drive. What would it be made of and why? What special features would be incorporated and why?

Take a Look

Bring in a couple of pairs of cowboy boots for inspection.

Discussion

Traditional cowboy boots were made of leather. It was easy to come by and could breathe so a cowboy's feet wouldn't get too hot or cold. The upper portion was covered with fancy stitching that kept the boots from folding over and causing irritation. The boots came up the calf to keep out pebbles and dirt and to protect the leg from underbrush. A narrow toe allowed the foot to slide easily in and out of the stirrups. Heels kept the foot from sliding through the stirrup and gave traction when a cowboy needed to dig in his heels to stop a runaway animal. Tabs, or mule ears, at the top of the boot, made it easy to pull the boots on.

Personalized Designer Cowboy Boot

Enlarge and photocopy this boot onto poster board. Have students cut it out and add stitching designs using a darning needle and wool, colored markers or puffy paint in squeeze bottles.

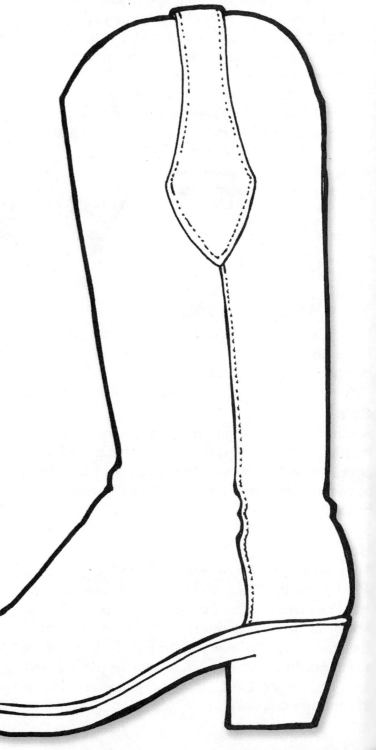

Name _____

Cowboy Gear Matchup

Match each item of a cowboy's gear to its name.

chaps	a large cotton handkerchief worn around the neck or pulled over the nose and mouth to keep out dust
stirrups	leather leg coverings tied over pants to protect and keep a rider warm
saddle	wide-brimmed headgear used to keep sun and rain off a cowboy's head and out of his eyes
bandanna	
spurs	the most important and expensive item a cowboy owned
lariat	protected a cowboy's feet and helped keep him balanced in the saddle
horseshoes	fitted over a horse's head with a bit for the mouth and reins that allowed a cowboy to guide the horse
bridle	
saddlebag	fitted over the back of the saddle to carry a cowboy's few belongings
cowboy hat	an important item for roping cattle
	small, blunt-edged or spiked wheels used to urge a horse on
	worn to protect a horse's hooves and legs

Cattle Drive

Ride 'em Cowboy

A cowboy had to train the wild horses he rode. He usually introduced a training bridle and saddle and then mounted the horse and let it buck until it wore itself out. Spurs and whips were sometimes used in training.

Materials
borrowed saddle and bridle
sawhorse with a 2' x 4' neck and head

What to Do
1. Secure a saddle over a sawhorse and attach a bridle to the "head."

2. Invite students to hop in the saddle. Talk about how it feels. What would it be like to sit in one all day? How would you direct the horse?

Guiding a Horse

Western horses were guided by neck reining. A cowboy held the reins in one hand and laid them on the left side of the horse's neck to make it turn right and on the right side of the neck to make it turn left. Spurs were sometimes used to make a horse move more quickly.

Tying Up Your Horse

Every cowboy knew how to tie a quick release knot that would unravel with the pull of the dangling end, even when a horse was pulling against it.

What to Do
Use red and black licorice whips to teach the tying of this knot. Once a knot has been successfully tied, a child can eat "the rope" and try again.

1. Loop one end of the rope over a railing (or broom handle or pointer suspended between two chairs). Have one student be the horse and hold one end of the rope.

2. Have the cowpoke bring the free end over the other to make a loop.

3. Form a loop with the free end and pull the second loop through the first loop and pull tightly.

4. Pull the dangling end. If your knot is tied properly, it will unravel.

Cattle Drive

Horse Sense

Cowboys could understand what horses were saying by the sounds they made and the way they moved. Can you?

What Is This Horse Saying?

"I am happy and relaxed."

"I am very interested in something. I am going to watch it carefully and decide what to do."

"I am angry, be careful."

"Watch out, I might kick."

"I am anxious, scared or worried."

"Hello, (or 'good-bye') friend"

How Many Hands High Are You?

Horses are measured in "hands" from the ground to the withers. A hand measures 4" (10.16 cm) across.

If you were a horse, how tall would you be?

Cattle Drive

Cow Ponies

A cowboy depended upon his horse to carry him along the trail day after day, up slopes, over rocky terrain, on cattle chases, through dense brush and blinding blizzards and sometimes across wide rivers. Cowboys liked small, hardy "hosses" who were fearless, intelligent, tough and fast.

Mustang

The hardy, surefooted mustang was small but powerful and made a great cow pony. This descendant of the magnificent Andalusian arrived with the Conquistadors from Spain and ran wild across the plains of America.

Quarter Horse

English horses were crossed with Spanish Andalusians by settlers of Virginia in the 17th century creating the first American breed of horse. The Quarter Horse is agile, hardy and capable of sudden bursts of speed making it useful for chasing and roping cattle.

Coloring and Markings

Horses come in many shades and colors. Color patterns on legs and faces are called markings. Cowboys liked horses with unique markings. Horses with spots are called pintos or paints, and an interesting horse with spots all over is called an appaloosa.

_____'s Cow Pony

Give your horse a little character using coloring and markings.

Cattle Drive

Cowboy Vittles

"Come and get it!" was a welcome sound at the end of a long day on the trail. A cook maintained and drove a chuck wagon along the trail and prepared a hot meal for 20 or so hungry cowboys every night. It was just about the same meal every night; sourdough biscuits, beans and buffalo or venison fried or cooked in a stew. Cowboys didn't eat the cattle they drove unless they had to. The meal ended with hot coffee and a simple dessert like apple pie if the cook wanted to keep the cowboys happy. After cooking and cleaning up supper, the cook pointed the tongue of the wagon in the direction of the North Star to provide a compass of sorts for the next morning's drive.

The chuck wagon was equipped with drawers and cubbies for storing staples such as flour, rice, salt, sugar, beans, coffee, baking powder, dried fruit and syrup. Cast iron pots and pans, a Dutch oven and utensils were stored or hinged for the rough ride. A water barrel was tied beneath the wagon and a hinged rear wall folded down to create a worktable.

Authentic Texas Cowboy Chili

Cook up an authentic cowboy dish with your students. Serve it in tin bowls with a side of sourdough biscuits. Chili made with cubed meat originated in San Antonio, Texas, as cooks found this a good way to serve tough Texas longhorn or wild game. This unique recipe will feed 25-30 little cowpokes.

Ingredients

10 lbs. (4.5 kg) beef (or venison) cubed
2 cloves fresh minced garlic
1/4 cup (60 ml) salt
1/2 cup (125 ml) chili powder
2 19-oz. (540 ml) cans both brown and kidney beans
2 T. (30 ml) ground pepper
1 medium onion
2 T. (30 ml) black pepper
1 cup (250 ml) flour
1/2 cup (125 ml) lard, shortening or butter— or cornstarch and water to thicken

What to Do

1. Place beef in a three-gallon cooking pot. Add water until the meat is just covered. Add remaining ingredients except for chili powder.

2. Bring to a boil and cook until meat is very tender.

3. Add chili powder and stir well. Remove from heat and set aside to cool.

4. Just before serving. Return to heat and thicken with a roux of two parts flour to one part lard—use only as much as needed.

Cattle Drive

Day Is Done

In the evening cowboys stopped to eat, drink and sleep along with their animals. Good food, good fellowship, hot coffee, quiet tunes, a card game or chance to read a book by a flickering fire and the swapping of tall tales were good ways to end a long, hard day.

Cowboys usually sat on the ground around a campfire. They didn't stay up late as they had to get an early start the next day. When the stars came out they took off their old boots and hats and crawled into the bedrolls they carried on their saddles. Some used their saddle or hat for a pillow. Whatever the weather, the cowboy worked, ate and slept under the wide-open sky—and what a sky it was. Historical references often comment on this wondrous sky.

Evening on the Trail Tableau

Have students create a tableau to represent a cowboy's evening on the trail.

What to Do
1. Encourage students to find out all they can about the cowboy's evening. Have students research activities and sounds of a particular territory.

2. Help students acquire and create items to add authenticity—a false campfire, cowboy attire, saddles, bedrolls, tin cups and coffeepot, old guitar, deck of cards.

3. Encourage students to create an *Evening on the Trail* soundtrack. Recording devices, CD ROM encyclopedia, cowboy music tape, etc., might be useful. (See Resources, page 5.)

Evening Sounds

Night sounds could be frightening to tenderfoots. Lying under the stars, cowboys might have heard wind rustling through the grasses, the wild howl of a wolf or yip of a coyote, the chirping of crickets, whining of mosquitoes, peeping of frogs, barking of a fox, blood-curdling screams of fighting raccoons, the gurgling of a creek or the far off thunder of an approaching storm.

Howl Like a Wolf or Yip Like a Coyote

Wolves howl to stake out territory, to find members of their pack, to talk to their babies, to signal a hunt or just for fun. Invite students to throw back their heads and let loose a long, deep, rolling howl or the repeated yips of a coyote.

Cattle Drive

What Would You Do at the End of the Trail?

When the noisy cattle filed into market or railroad towns, they were taken to pens for sale or slaughter or to railcars for the next leg of their journey. Once the cattle were in their pens the cowboys got their pay.

- Imagine how you would feel if you were a cowboy, after weeks or months on the dusty trail. What would you do at the end of the trail, in a market town, with money in your pocket?

The end of the trail was a time for fun, rest and relaxation before the next adventure. The first things a cowboy usually wanted were a bath, a shave and a haircut. Barbers offered big tubs where tired, dirty cowboys could soak all they wanted for a fee. Next came a civilized meal at a table, using a chair, and then maybe shopping for new gear before socializing on the town with a little singing and dancing, maybe gambling and drinking and a good night's sleep in a real bed.

Settle on the Ranch?

For some the end of the trail was an open-range ranch. Here the cattle were left to graze while the cowboys were welcomed into the bunkhouse for some cowboy hospitality. By the late 1800s these ranches were springing up in the northwestern United States and Western Canada. Ranching was becoming very profitable and some ranchers owned thousands of cattle and thousands of acres of land. Cowboys whose trail ended at a ranch often chose to stay on and work there.

The End of the Cattle Drives

The incredible journey of cattle across the open range was a short but spectacular time in history. It is estimated that between 1865 and 1885 over 10 million cattle were sold and over 40,000 cowboys hired in North America. By the late 1880s falling beef prices, competition for land and water, a movement of settlers and sheep farmers to the new frontier and the installation of barbed wire around sprawling ranches brought an end to this era. Violent confrontations, summer droughts and winter storms brought the final blow to the era of open-range ranching, and by 1890 the days of cowboy trail drives across the open range were over.

Cattle Drive

The Rodeo

The rodeo has lived on from the days of the cattle drives when cowboys engaged in competitions when they met on the trail or at the trailhead. Friendly challenges gave cowpokes the opportunity to measure their cow handling skills against those of others. By the 1880s rodeos had become organized gatherings with specific events and rules and by the 1900s some cowboys made following the rodeo circuit a profession. The famous Calgary Stampede, in Calgary, Canada, began in 1912 and is going strong to this day. There are even rodeos just for kids, like the Little Britches Rodeo held in California.

Rodeo events feature skills cowhands use on the job. Saddle and bareback bronc riding reflect the challenges of taming wild horses. Steer wrestling is the ultimate test in cow handling and horsemanship. Calf roping relies on skills needed to catch a calf, while barrel racing tests the speed and agility needed to cut a cow from the herd.

Roundup Rodeo

Have a rodeo instead of gym class! Invite students to create activities based on skills and activities of the cattle drive.

Bull in the Pen

How to Play

1. Have players form a circle. Choose one player to be the Bull.

2. The Bull goes to the center of the ring. He will attempt to break through the joined hands of players who form the circle around him.

3. When the Bull escapes, he or she chooses one of the players from the broken chain to become the next Bull.

Roundup

How to Play

1. Mark off a designated "open range" with reasonable boundaries.

2. Choose one or two children to be the Cowhands. Other players become Longhorns and must hold their arms out to their sides to indicate horns.

3. On a signal, Cowhands chase and tag Longhorns within the boundaries.

4. When Longhorns are tagged, they become Cowhands and drop their "horns." The new Cowhands help to tag the remaining Longhorns.

5. Play continues until all Longhorns have been "rounded up."

Cattle Drive

Come to the Cattle Drive

Host a cattle drive as a culminating event to this unit. Invite parents or other students in the school to learn about life on the trail as your students share new skills, knowledge and projects.

Cowboy Campfire

Set the scene with an end-of-the-trail campfire using an electric log set or flashlights and colored paper. Make authentic benches using straw bales, barn board and plywood. Throw in wagon wheels and horsy gear for ambiance.

- Have children share their cowboy choruses, poetry and tall tales around the fire.

- Invite guests to bring guitars, harmonicas and their ability to carry a tune. Lead the cowhands in some old favorites like "Red River Valley," "Sweet Betsy from Pike," "Whoopee Ti-Yi-Yo" and "Home on the Range."

Display Cowboy Creations

Decorate the gym or your classroom with "cattle drive" projects and artwork.

Come in Cowboy Get-Up

Invite guests to dress for the occasion. Have students explain why they are dressed as they are. A pair of blue jeans was sturdy and simple, a button-up shirt common and cool (in cotton, plaid or wool), a pair of boots and a cotton bandanna were practical. Encourage cowboys to explain why their hats, boots and bandannas were so important on the trail.

Cowboy Characters

Invite students and guests to research and become characters from the Old West. Suggest "Cookie" the common name for the chuck wagon cook, a wrangler, a flank rider, a trail boss or Joseph McCoy a Yankee stockman who instigated the movement of cattle across the continent by building a stockyard and hotel in Abilene, Texas. Girls might consider Annie Oakley, star of Buffalo Bill's Wild West Show (1883-1916). She performed tricks while standing on the back of a galloping horse in a short fringed dress. She was never a real cowgirl although she created the image many associate with cowgirls. Cowgirls didn't make it to the range until after the cattle drives.

Cattle Drive

Cowboy Speak

If you are using words from the cowboys' vocabulary, you are probably speaking Spanish. North American cowboys adopted much of their language from the Spanish-speaking Mexican vaqueros. Invite students to make their own Cowboy Dictionaries using new words they have learned in this unit.

amigo: from the Spanish word meaning "friend"

bean time: beans were so common at meals that mealtime came to be known by this term

buckaroo: from the Spanish word *vaquero*, meaning "cowboy." In Spanish the letter V is pronounced as our B sound. Early cowboys pronounced *vaquero* as "buckaroo."

chaps: tie-on leather leg protectors, from *chaperejos* for leg armor

chuck: food made on the chuck wagon and eaten on the trail

cinch: the strap that goes under a horse's belly to keep the saddle in place

lariat: a rope with a running noose used for roping cattle, from the word *la reata* meaning "the rope"

maverick: a calf that does not have a brand

pinto: a spotted horse, from the word *pinto* meaning "spotted or speckled"

ranch: from *rancho* meaning "camp or small farm"

rawhide: the skin of an animal before it is treated to become leather

stampede: a scattering of cattle or horses, from the word *stampede* meaning "pounding or loud sound"

steer: a bull that has been fixed so it cannot father offspring

tenderfoot: a new cowboy

Adios, partner!